REAPPRAISING INDIA'S LOOK EAST POLICY

TIME FOR A HUMAN SECURITY ORIENTED AGENDA

Shantanu Chakrabarti

KNOWLEDGE WORLD
KW Publishers Pvt Ltd
New Delhi

The Court of Directors of the East India Company sent a despatch in July, 1854 to the Governor-General of India in Council, suggesting the establishment of the Universities of Calcutta, Madras and Bombay.

In pursuance of that despatch, the University of Calcutta was founded on January 24, 1857.

The University adopted in the first instance, the pattern of the University of London and gradually introduced modifications in its constitution.

ISBN 978-93-80502-66-3

KNOWLEDGE WORLD

Published in India by

Kalpana Shukla
KW Publishers Pvt Ltd
4676/21, First Floor, Ansari Road, Daryaganj, New Delhi 110002
Phone: +91.11.23263498 / 43528107
email: mail@kwpub.in / knowledgeworld@vsnl.net

Printed and Bound in India

CONTENTS

1. Adopting the Correct Approach 2
2. Historical Background 3
3. Structural Integration 6
4. Bilateral Engagements 9
5. Strategic Factors in 'Look East Policy' 14
6. The Northeast Connection 16
7. Evolving a Long-term Strategy Based on Human Security Paradigm? 18
8. Concluding Remarks 21

Reappraising India's 'Look East Policy': Time For A Human Security-Oriented Agenda

India's expanding links with the countries located in Southeast Asia and East Asia along with her burgeoning influence in the Asia–Pacific and Indian ocean zones since the 1990s have come under the collective analytical framework of 'Look East Policy,' and have been scrutinised and analysed from every possible scholarly dimension over the years.[1] Over the last two decades the policy has received official sanctification and confirmation and has been mentioned in almost every public document issued by the concerned departments and agencies of the Indian government. That in itself is, however, no guarantee as to the degree of 'maturity' or sophistication which the policy might have acquired over the period. Most of the scholarly writings on the 'Look East Policy', in fact, adopt critical tones when discussing the issue either finding fault with government policies or lacuna in global and regional geopolitics hampering proper implementation of the policy. 'Look East Policy', however, has been evolving over time. When initiated during the 1990s as a government directed policy, the primary focus was on improving economic relations with the 'tiger economies' in the Southeast Asia. Subsequently, the policy has evolved into a more complex one (sometimes referred to as Phase-II) through extension of focus into Asia–Pacific and Indian ocean region; combining economics with strategic dimension whether in terms of projection of Indian naval power in India ocean and even in the South China sea region; a perceptible competition with China over the question of Asian leadership; and, triggering growth and development in the Indian Northeast region as a key element in the overall policy making. The purpose of this paper is to attempt a reappraisal of India's Look East as it has evolved through these various twists and turns trying to find out whether it has developed a degree of strategic coherence and whether it would be appropriate to recast and project it within an alternative 'human security' oriented paradigm.

Adopting the Correct Approach

Scholars analysing India's 'Look East Policy', either adopt a minimalist position focusing on the evolution of this policy as a contemporary phenomenon particularly since the 1990s or a maximalist or 'longue duree' approach focusing on the long-term cycles of historical periods of engagement. A 'minimalist' analyst, for instance, remarks:

"...Look East and its associated strategies to establish India's presence in Asia have become an institutionalized component of the country's foreign policy. This approach has met with success because it achieves important foreign policy goals for both India and its partners. Increased engagement in the region is part of New Delhi's overall effort to increase its presence in an area where its sphere of influence overlaps with that of Beijing. For ASEAN member countries, India provides an alternative that allows them to reduce their economic dependence on both China and Japan. Unlike those two East Asian powers, India does not have a historical legacy of invasion or domination in the region. Deeper integration with India allows ASEAN nations to tap into a dynamic liberalizing economy in a democratic state." [2]

The 'longue duree' approach, on the other hand, adopted by another scholar, argues that for a proper perspective on India's substantial engagement with the east, one has to identify at least four different waves of such engagement namely, historical or pre-colonial, colonial, post-colonial, and contemporary. [3] The long-term historical approach provides a scholar with better analytical tools and a better understanding of the evolving patterns of relationships at various levels between the various Asian regions particularly the interconnections in the commercial and cultural spheres. Contemporary and current developments do not always follow the set historical patterns as evolved in the past, but nonetheless, can help us in contextualizing the present developments in order to improve our understanding of the phenomenon.

At present, for instance, India and ASEAN(Association of Southeast Asian Nations) have shown a degree of convergence in their security perspectives. India have developed vital stakes in peace and stability in the region, including the security of the sea-lanes of the Indian Ocean for smooth flow of raw materials, merchandise, and energy supplies.[4] One, however, also has to remember that there is no uniformity in Southeast Asian perception of India and China's rise. The regional diversities and the different degrees of perception among Southeast Asians have been mainly determined by factors like the geographical proximity, historical context, stage of economic development, political, and social orientation and web of complex political and security arrangements with other powers.[5]

Historical Background

India has geographical proximity to Southeast Asia, sharing its maritime boundary with at least three countries, the closeness of Andaman and Nicobar Islands in the Bay of Bengal to Southeast Asia than to mainland India and the fact that southern Indian tip is astride some of the most important sea lanes of communication in the Indian Ocean, connecting Southeast Asia (and East Asia) with West Asia and Europe through which nearly 40 per cent of the world's trade passes through.[6] Naturally, this has given rise to civilizational contacts in various spheres and at various levels between the two regions developed over the historical period. Pilgrimage, economic and trade voyages and sometimes armed missions throughout the historical period have deepened such relationships.

The Indian subcontinent had also formed an integral part of the economic and cultural networks interconnecting the Asian continent. According to historian Sugata Bose, for instance:

In early times, the thriving agrarian and urban economies of the Achaemenid and Mauryan empires provided the basis for the exchanges between the Middle East and South Asia, which predated the crafting of close links between South and Southeast Asia. By the beginning of the common era, there was a perceptible shift in the balance, from the earlier emphasis on luxuries, to staple goods in the commodity composition of the Indian Ocean trade. At key centers throughout this realm sprang up important expatriate communities of South Asian merchants, who appear to have been more direct agents of cultural diffusion in Southeast Asia than in the Middle East.[7]

Such contacts continued to flower during the later period particularly from the Gupta period up to the period of the Chola Empire in early medieval period. The advent of Islam added another dimension to these patterns of contact. According to Fernand Braudel, for instance, in pre-colonial period the Far-East consisted of the three large and interconnected world economies: Islam, overlooking the Indian Ocean from the Red Sea and the Persian Gulf, and controlling the endless chain of deserts stretching across Asia from Arabia to China; India, whose influence extended throughout the Indian Ocean, both east and west of Cape Comorin; and China, at once a great territorial power—striking deep into the heart of Asia—and a maritime force, controlling the seas and countries bordering the Pacific.[8] Advent of colonial powers did to an extent disrupt the traditional linkages but not to the extent as was once believed.[9] Modern analysts have shown that colonial powers like the Portuguese, the Dutch and the French and the English had to make adjustments and co-opt the indigenous and traditional linkages to an extent.

Under British colonialism, there were certain attempts to project India as as major strategic centre of Britain's Afro-Asian empire. Viceroy Lord Curzon(1899–1905), for instance, going beyond Viceroy Lord Mayo's(1869–1872) conception of an 'informal empire,' often taking a strong line against the strategic thinking of the policymakers in London, highlighted his grand vision of treating India as the, " important strategic location with major resources and the point from which British interests in the Middle East, Southeast Asia and China could be controlled."[10] He was, however, not particularly successful.

Keeping pace with improvements in communication and transport networks, the colonial period would also witness greater and more diverse patterns of migration of Indian indigenous communities in all parts of the world including Southeast Asia and China. These would include merchants and other commercial groups, soldiers, policemen, labourers, and also educated middle class in search of white collar jobs. At the time of Indian independence in 1947, large numbers of Indian immigrants were living in Southeast Asia and the Indian Ocean islands.

Re-engagement with Asia, as far possible on Indian terms, was, thus, very much a part of Nehru's foreign policy agenda. Speaking in the Constituent Assembly of India on 8 March 1949, Nehru said:

When we talk of Asia, remember that India, not because of any ambition of hers, but because of the force of circumstances, because of geography, because of history and because of so many other things, inevitably has to play a very important part in Asia...India becomes a kind of meeting ground for various trends and forces and a meeting ground between what might roughly be called the East and the West...If you have to consider any question affecting the Middle East, India inevitably comes into the picture. If you have to consider any question concerning South-East Asia, you cannot do so without India. So also with the Far East...Even if you think in terms of regional organizations in Asia, you have to keep in touch with the other regions. And whatever regions you may have in mind, the importance of India cannot be ignored. [11]

Nehru's efforts in this regard via the Asian relations conferences in 1947 and in 1949 and through the Bandung experiment of 1955 did not have much impact. Cold War dynamics and the rise of People's Republic of China generated divisions in Asia which would witness India and most of the Southeast Asian countries on opposite ends. During the late 1950s and early 1960s India had good diplomatic relations with Indonesia, but the other countries of the region did not receive much attention of the South Block in New Delhi. [12]

The characteristic feature of this phase of India's 'Look East Policy' was decolonisation and Asian resurgence. Both of these aspects were primarily emotional and ideological in content. The Nehruvian vision had a strong political content to back them but was bereft of much tangible substance; of commerce, culture, and economy, as was evident during the first wave period. Nor was much attention paid, save rhetorical recognition, to the security imperatives of the developments in Indian Ocean, except during the late sixties and early seventies when India encouraged and backed the proposals for reducing the scale of arms race in the Indian Ocean by getting it recognised as a 'Zone of Peace.' [13]

India under Indira Gandhi also associated itself with the process of the formation of ASEAN during 1966–67. It worked intensely for evolving a broad-based regional organisation of cooperation, which did not identify itself with any of the superpowers' strategic and Cold War-oriented interests. This did not succeed and the result was an ASEAN representing an ideologically and strategically divided Southeast Asia in which India had no place. [14] When Malaysia invited New Delhi as a full dialogue partner twice in 1975 and again in 1980, she was disinterested. [15] India actually missed its second chance with the ASEAN in 1980. In May 1980, following a meeting between Indian and ASEAN officials in Kuala Lumpur, a framework for a 'step-by-step' cooperation between India and ASEAN as a group was agreed on, covering economic areas, specifically trade, international economic cooperation, industrial cooperation, and scientific and technological cooperation. However, the pursuance of this agreement was vitiated when India, ignoring ASEAN's collective position on Kampuchea, recognised the Hang Samrin regime that was seen as a protégé of Vietnam. Realising that ASEAN would not approve of this action, India's then foreign minister Narasimha Rao avoided participating in the ASEAN meeting in July 1980. ASEAN also did not bother to invite India subsequently. [16]

Under the premiership of Rajiv Gandhi, certain steps were taken during the late 1980s in reviving India's relations with its eastern neighbours. There was a sudden spurt in diplomatic exchanges between India and the countries of Southeast Asia during the five years (1985–89) of Rajiv Gandhi's tenure along with rapprochement achieved with China. [17]

Thus, the 'Look East Policy' initiated under Prime Minister Narasimha Rao during the 1990s did not occur in a vacuum but had a long historical background as well as more contemporaneous context. The financial crisis of the early 1990s and the geopolitical crisis generated by the collapse of the Soviet Union in 1991 also acted as crucial factors in India's attempts to reach out and engage new areas and regions. Southeast Asia and the Asia–Pacific region were obvious choices given the geographical proximity, historic background, opportunity provided by the ending of Cold War determined regional relationship patterns and, the robust nature of the Asian 'tiger economies.'

Structural Integration

India has now accepted that its economic destiny is now firmly linked to its fuller integration in the global economy. However, such global integration will come increasingly through greater connectivity and enmeshing with the dynamic economies of Southeast Asia and East Asia. [18]

'Look East Policy', a part of India's extended neighbourhood policy was initiated by the then Prime Minister Narasimha Rao in his Singapore address in 1994 and has been vigorously followed by successive governments providing a degree of consistency and stability.

This has involved series of engagements at bilateral levels as well as multilateral negotiations in regional forums and organisations. India had become a sectoral dialogue partner of the ASEAN in 1992 and a full-fledged dialogue partner in 1995. In 1996, India joined the ASEAN Regional Forum (ARF). India-ASEAN Summits are being regularly held since 2002. In 2003, India became one of the first non-Southeast Asian nations to accede to ASEAN's Treaty of Amity and Cooperation, which commits India to upholding the provisions of ASEAN's 1967 charter. ASEAN and India also signed a Joint Declaration for Cooperation in Combating International Terrorism, symbolising concrete initiatives to step up cooperation in the fight against terrorism. India rushing in with help immediately after the tsunami in 2004 generated a great deal of goodwill in the Southeast and Indian Ocean rim countries. ASEAN subsequently formed another regional organisation called the ASEAN Defence Ministers Meeting (ADMM) in 2007 to cooperate in the areas of humanitarian and disaster relief. At its fourth meeting in Singapore in May 2010, the ADMM became ADMM + 8, by including eight other members namely Japan, Korea, China, Australia, New Zealand, India, Russia, and the United States. The first meeting of the expanded ADMM took place in Vietnam in October 2010. India also became a founding member of the East Asia Summit(EAS) in 2005.

Apart from rising trade there has been a steady flow of investments both ways. Foreign direct investment net inflow to ASEAN from India amounted to US $983.6 million.[19] Mauritius, Singapore, and Japan now figure among the top ten FDI sources to India.[20] India was also placed among the top ten sources of tourists visiting ASEAN countries with better air connectivity being developed.

At the Second ASEAN-India Summit in 2003, the ASEAN-India Framework Agreement on Comprehensive Economic Cooperation was signed. As part of the Comprehensive Economic Cooperation Agreement, the ASEAN-India Free Trade in Goods Agreement was signed in 2009 and came into effect from 1 January 2010. ASEAN and India are currently working towards the early conclusion of the ASEAN-India Trade in Services and Investment Agreements. During the negotiations India has reportedly made requests to open up several service areas, including teaching, nursing, architecture, chartered accountancy, and medicine. India is also keen on expanding its telecoms, information technology, tourism, and banking network in ASEAN countries.[21] The ASEAN region is a net importer of services, buying nearly US $180 billion worth of services in 2007. In view of this and India's competitive advantages in terms of cost and expertise in a range of areas, such increased access will be very beneficial.[22]

Integration has also involved widening and deepening of engagement. Widening of engagement has been a part of the so called 'Phase-II' part of the engagement in trying to extend linkages with East Asian countries and organisations along with greater engagement with the Asia–Pacific islands in the South and in the Indian Ocean zone. The three important regional organisations in this sphere are the IOR-ARC, the BIMSTEC and the Ganga Mekong Cooperation. The Indian Ocean Rim Association for Regional Cooperation (IOR-ARC) was formed in 1997 as a tripartite structure which brings together representatives of government, business, and the academic world for promoting regional cooperation. It is currently a 19 member body consisting of Australia, Bangladesh, India, Indonesia, Iran, Kenya, Madagascar, Malaysia, Mauritius, Mozambique, Oman, the Seychelles, Singapore, South Africa, Sri Lanka, Tanzania, Thailand, the United Arab Emirates, and Yemen. China, Egypt, France, Japan, and the United Kingdom are dialogue partners. IOR-ARC activities include several on-going topical projects and work programs conducted by member countries of shared interests, all of which under the umbrella of three separate working groups, namely the Working Group on Trade and Investment (WGTI), the Indian Ocean Rim Business Forum (IORBF), and the Indian Ocean Rim Academic Group (IORAG). The Association holds a Council of Ministers meeting once every two years.[23]

The BISTEC ((Bangladesh, India, Sri Lanka, and Thailand Economic Cooperation) formed in 1997 was renamed as BIMSTEC with the joining of Myanmar in the organisation. Subsequently Nepal and Bhutan also joined the group. The association was subsequently renamed as the Bay of Bengal Initiative for Multi-Sectoral Technical and Economic Cooperation. BIMSTEC was initiated with the goal to combine the 'Look West Policy' of Thailand and ASEAN with the 'Look East Policy' of India and South Asia. So it could be explained that BIMSTEC is a link between ASEAN and South Asian Association for Regional Cooperation (SAARC). Seven members of BIMSTEC covers 13 priority sectors lead by member countries in a voluntary manner namely, Trade & Investment, Technology, Energy, Transport & Communication, Tourism, Fisheries, Agriculture, Cultural Cooperation, Environment and Disaster Management, Public Health, People-to-People Contract, Poverty Alleviation, and Counter-Terrorism and Transnational Crimes.[24]

Mekong-Ganga Cooperation (MGC) was established on 10 November 2000 at Vientiane in the First MGC Ministerial Meeting. It comprises of six member countries namely, Thailand, Myanmar, Cambodia, Lao PDR, Vietnam, and India. The emphases are on four areas of cooperation, which are tourism, culture, education, and transportation linkage in order to be solid foundation for future trade and investment cooperation in the region.

Bilateral Engagements

The special focus on the new ASEAN entrants during the 1990s in India's 'Look East Policy' has, over the past years, also led to the creation of a separate administrative unit, the CLMV (Cambodia, Laos, Myanmar, and Vietnam) desk, in the Ministry of External Affairs to deal with them. Special programmes of assistance and cooperation in diverse fields are being initiated and executed in CLMV (Cambodia, Laos, Myanmar, and Vietnam) countries through this unit.[25]

Bilateral engagement with older members within the ASEAN has also been steady.

- Singapore—Singapore is India's largest trade and investment partner in ASEAN. India's export value stood at US $7,592.17 million in 2009–2010 while import value amounted to US $6,454.57 million. Economic and commercial ties between the two countries have expanded significantly, particularly after the conclusion of the Comprehensive Economic Cooperation Agreement (CECA) in 2005.[26] Singapore is the second largest FDI investor in India. Singapore also has a burgeoning defence relationship with India. Annual naval exercises conducted by the two navies. There are existing training programmes for Singaporean defence personnel in India.

- Malaysia—Malaysia is the second largest trading partner for India within ASEAN, and India is the largest trading partner for Malaysia from among the countries of the South, excluding China. Indian export figure to Malaysia stood at US $2,835.41million during 2009–2010 and the import amounted to US $5,176.78 million. With the coming into force of the ASEAN-India FTA in Goods from 1 January 2010, the bilateral economic engagement is expected to get a further fillip in the coming years. India and Malaysia have signed an agreement signalling the conclusion of negotiations on a CECA as a single undertaking covering goods, services, investment, and other areas of cooperation.[27]
- Indonesia—Indian export to Indonesia stood at US $3,063.36 million and import US $8,656.66 million during 2009–2010. India is Indonesia's largest buyer of Crude Palm Oil (CPO) and an importer of its minerals (particularly coal and copper ore). India and Indonesia have concluded a study on a bilateral CECA with Indonesia and an announcement on the commencement of CECA negotiations was made during the recent visit of President Yudhoyono to India. The two countries signed a Defence Cooperation Agreement in 2001 and have had regular defence exchanges.[28]
- Thailand—Over the past two decades India's 'Look East Policy' has been complemented by Thailand's 'Look West Policy'. They cooperate closely in the ASEAN, East Asia Summit (EAS) and BIMSTEC groupings as also Mekong Ganga Cooperation (MGC) and Asia Cooperation Dialogue (ACD). The implementation of the India-AESAN Agreement on Trade in Goods from January 2010 is an important latest milestone of this partnership.[29] Indian export figure stood at US $1,740.16 million while import value stood at US $2,931.52 million.
- Vietnam—Vietnam is an important regional partner in Southeast Asia.

India and Vietnam closely cooperate in various regional forums such as ASEAN, East Asia Summit and the Mekong Ganga Cooperation. India figures among the ten largest exporters to Vietnam. With the signing of the India-ASEAN FTA on Trade in Goods, bilateral trade with Vietnam is poised to grow faster. Vietnam has recently ratified the India-ASEAN FTA in Goods w.e.f 1 June 2010.[30] Indian exports US $1,838.95 million while import figure was US $521.81 million (2009–2010). A Memorandum of Understanding (MoU) on defence cooperation was signed by the two countries on 5 November 2009.

- Philippines—Trade has more than trebled from US $338.50 million in 2001–02 to US $ 1061.84 million in 2009–10.[31] Indian export value stood at US $748.77 million while import amounted to US $313.07 million in 2009–2010. Negotiations are being held to expand defence related cooperation also.
- Laos PDR—Indian exports to the Lao PDR primarily consist of agriculture machinery, irrigation pumps, raw-material for garments, drugs and pharmaceuticals, machinery, paints and varnishes, textiles, and sports and electrical goods. Lao exports to India consist mainly of fragrant wood used for agarbattis and other agro-based products. Two-way trade in 2009–10 was worth US $37 million, a 288% increase over the previous year.[32] Indian export figure stood at US $16.93 million while import amounted to US $20.05 million.
- Brunei—Till 2002, bilateral trade and economic cooperation remained between the two countries remained rather limited. In 2003, bilateral trade increased substantially with the commencement of import of crude oil by India from Brunei, and the export of IT products from India to Brunei.[33] Indian export figure stood at US $24.44 million whereas the import figure was US $428.65 million during 2009–10.
- Cambodia—After the collapse of Khmer Rouge regime, India recognised the Heng Samrin regime and opened its Embassy in Phnom Penh in 1981 when much of the world had shunned Cambodia. This factor along with India's association with the Paris Peace Accords and their finalisation in 1991 has generated a lot of goodwill for India. India also committed military and non-military personnel for the conduct of the

UNTAC-sponsored elections in 1993.[34] Indian export amounted to US $45.54 million (2009–2010) and import value was US $5.05 million.

- Myanmar—India and Myanmar share a long land border of over 1600 km and a maritime boundary in the Bay of Bengal. From a strategic point of view, India's 'Look East Policy' has to be strategised through Myanmar as this is the only country within the ASEAN with which India shares a common border. India and Myanmar signed a border trade agreement in 1994 and have two operational border trade points (Moreh-Tamu and Zowkhatar—Rhi on the 1664 km long border). Agreement has also been reached on setting up a third border trade point at Avakhung-Pansat/Somra.[35] Indian exports amounted to US $207.97 million in 2009–2010 while import amounted to US $1,289.80 million.

Widening of engagement process has also involved India continuing her focus on social and economic assistance programme while maintaining cordial ties with Fiji Islands, Tonga, Tuvalu, and Cook Islands, in line with its 'Look East Policy'. [36] The tables given below provide some glimpses of the range of economic interests involved in the 'Look East Policy'.

Table 1: India's Trade Linkages in Look East Policy

S.No.	Country	Export from India (2005-2006) (US $ Million)	Export from India (2009-2010) (US $ Million)	Import by India(2005-2006) (US $ Million)	Import by India(2009-2010) (US $ Million)
ASEAN					
1	Brunei	42.94	24.44	0.88	428.65
2	Cambodia	24.19	45.54	0.78	5.05
3	Indonesia	1,380.20	3,063.36	3,008.11	8,656.66
4	Laos PDR	5.47	16.93	0.10	20.05
5	Malaysia	1,161.86	2,835.41	2,415.61	5,176.78
6	Myanmar	110.70	207.97	525.96	1,289.80
7	Philippines	494.66	748.77	235.49	313.07
8	Singapore	5,425.29	7,592.17	3,353.77	6,454.57
9	Thailand	1,075.31	1,740.16	1,211.58	2,931.52

10	Vietnam	690.68	1,838.95	131.39	521.81
East Asia					
1	China	6,759.10	11,617.88	10,868.05	30,824.02
2	Japan	2,481.26	3,629.54	4,061.10	6,734.18
3	Mongolia	1.17	7.98	1.62	1.26
4	North Korea	54.53	422.38	56.57	8.71
3	South Korea	1,827.21	3,421.05	4,563.85	8,576.07
Australia & New Zealand					
1	Australia	821.23	1,384.96	4,947.91	12,407.37
2	New Zealand	141.90	255.17	216.63	499.21
Pacific Islands					
1.	Fiji Islands	29.06	26.69	0.85	1.34
2.	Tonga	0.44	0.49	0.11	0.00
3.	Tuvalu	0.14	0.21	0.00	0.05
4.	Cook Islands	0.09	0.03	0.01	-

Source: Export-Import Data Bank, Department of Commerce, Ministry of Commerce and Industry, Government of India (http://commerce.nic.in/eidb/iecntq.asp)(accessed: 21 February 2011)

Table 2: Indian Major Business Entities at South East Asia

Indian Major Business Entities at South East Asia	
Indian MNCs	Operating in South East Asian Nations
Reddy's Lab, Ranbaxy, Tata steel	Cambodia
Jindal Steel, Crompton Greaves, Punj Llyod, Tata steel	Indonesia
Reliance Industries, Tata Steel, Reddy's Lab, Ranbaxy, GMR Infrastructure, Punj Llyod, Tata steel, Reliance	Malaysia
Tata Steel, Reddy's Lab, Ranbaxy	Myanmar
NASSCOM, GMR Infrastructure, Tata steel	Philippines

Reddy's Lab, Ranbaxy, Tata Steel, Infosys, Wipro, BSNL, Kirloskar, Bharti-Televenture, Glaxo, NASSCOM, Punj Llyod, Sun Pharma, Tata Steel, Reliance	Singapore
Aditya Birla Group, Ballarpur Industries, Baroda Rayon Group, Usha Martin Industries, Ranbaxy Laboratories, Lupin Laboratories, Bharat Overseas Bank, Indo-Rama Groups, Punj Lyod, Tata Steel	Thailand
Essar Steel, ONGC, Punj Llyod (Petro-Vietnam), Sun Pharma, Tata steel, Reliance	Vietnam
Tata steel	Laos

Source: Table 1, 'Indian Major Business Entities at South East Asia' in Arup Barman and Ramananda Singh, Growing Interconnections between India and ASEAN-10- An Essay on Depth of Trade Collaboration, p.3 (http://zunia.org/ uploads/ media/ knowledge/ The% 20 Growing% 20Interconnection% 20between% 20 India % 20and%20ASEAN%20_ Repaired_1280227901.pdf(accessed: 26 February 2011).

One of the core concern within the 'Look East policy'-making process focuses on the growing economic convergence with key Southeast and East Asian countries at bilateral levels and also through integration within regional set ups. At another level, however, the 'Look East Policy' would continue its 'widening' and 'deepening' initiatives essentially as strategic and political initiatives even when economically not very viable. Such trends seem to be more visible and overt in recent years.

Strategic Factors in 'Look East Policy'

At a geo-strategic level, after the end of the Cold War, it became increasingly untenable, illogical, and detrimental to India's long-term national interests to continue to regard South Asia and Southeast Asia as separate strategic theatres. [37]

As one scholar notes that "... *(t) he global financial crisis and the decisive shift in the balance of the global economy should convince India about engaging the East more vigorously, both economically and strategically."* [38] India's unspoken goal, beyond the promotion of its economic interests (which has at times been strongly supported by some East and Southeast Asian nations), seems to be to manage, and, where necessary, counter, rising Chinese influence that might both encircle it and undermine its aspirations to a meaningful leadership role within the Asian continent and globally. [39] The desire to extend India's strategic influence in the region has primarily been sought to be achieved through defence cooperation and tie ups along with the increase of the Indian naval's presence in the region. The 'Look East Policy' initiative in this connection fits within the overall Indian aspirations to become the regional hegemon of South Asia and the Indian Ocean Region, and an extra-regional power in the Middle East, Central Asia, and Southeast Asia.[40]

One of the earliest Indian defence agreements in the region had been with Mauritius. Mauritius has a defence agreement that has been in place since 1974 whereby the Indian Navy provides military leadership to the Mauritius Coast Guard on deputation. India has also transferred naval vessels and equipment to Mauritius over the years.[41] Since 1991, India has also periodically held joint naval exercises with Singapore, Malaysia, and Indonesia in the Indian ocean. In subsequent years, it has undertaken bilateral exercises with Vietnam, Thailand, and the Philippines.[42] The multinational naval exercise MILAN with navies from Southeast countries and Asia–Pacific region are periodically held in the Bay of Bengal area. In 2005 a Far Eastern Naval Command (FENC) was established at Port Blair in the Andaman Islands, which is located midway between the Bay of Bengal and the Straits of Malacca—a key chokepoint linking the Indian Ocean to the South China sea. By 2012 it is expected that the FENC will consist of three main bases and a network of anchor stations that will house surface combatants and patrol vessels as well as submarines.[43] Coordinated patrol in collaboration with Indonesia (named INDINDO CORPAT) along the International Maritime Boundary Line (IMBL) between India and Indonesia has been continuing twice a year since its inception in 2002.[44] Training of armed staff from countries like Singapore, Indonesia are also being done on a regular basis. India's defence ties with Japan have been evolving over the recent years. Exchange of high-level visits and training courses have been the highlights of India-Japan defence cooperation. The trilateral exercise named 'Malabar CY 09' involving Indian Navy, US Navy, and Japan Maritime Self Defence Force was held off Okinawa from 26 April to 3 May 2009. [45]

Another strategic development which has gone somewhat unnoticed is India's growing presence in Southeast and East Asia been reciprocated by growing East Asian involvement in South Asian regional development. East Asian countries like China, Japan, and South Korea have acquired observer status in SAARC. Japan has also involved herself in Sri Lanka. Japan had provided aid during the last stages of Civil War in Sri Lanka. Japan also sent peacekeepers to Nepal to monitor the ceasefire between the government and the Maoist rebels. Greater Chinese involvement in South Asia and the Indian ocean zone, through Bangladesh, Myanmar, Sri Lanka have been viewed by India as part of a 'string of pearls' strategy of economic and military encroachment into South and Central Asia.[46] Chinese 'all weather' strategic partnership with Pakistan also has generated concerns for the Indian policy makers.

China has primarily adopted a cautious policy in her assessment of India's recent initiatives in the realm of 'Look East Policy'. Chinese analysts are increasingly venting critical views of India trying to use its 'Look East Policy' as a strategic goal not only to expand its influence in Southeast Asia but also in East Asia particularly by the possibility of creating a strategic partnership with Japan *vis a vis* an expanding China. One columnist writing in the People's Daily Online version, for instance, cautions that:

India's "Look East policy" was born out of failure—the failure of India's Cold War strategy of "playing both ends against the middle", today, India is harping on the same string, but should wisely skip the out-of-tune piece. [47]

It has also been argued that India's strategic capability in the region essentially still remains rather limited and apart from its participation in the ARF dialogues and occasional forays into the Straits of Malacca for patrolling in combating piracy, India unfortunately is still an insignificant player in the security structure of the region. [48]

The Northeast Connection

Inspite of the physical proximity and the ethnic linkages and ties, the Indian policy makers have largely failed in involving the Northeast region within the 'Look East Policy' making structure. An admission to this effect was made by the then External Affairs Minister, Shri Pranab Mukherjee in his statement that:

"...(W)e have felt for some time the need to focus the benefits of this cooperation more sharply on our Northeastern region, which is a natural bridge between India and Southeast Asia [49]

The release of the Northeast Vision 2020 document in 2008 was supposed to address this lacuna and provide a guideline for greater involvement of the region in the 'Look East Policy' making. The document states that:

The immediate priority is to build the required infrastructure right up to the border areas, establishing connectivity and communication links to the cross-border points through which trade and economic exchanges with the countries neighbouring the North Eastern Region are proposed to be promoted under the Look East Policy. This priority is to be accorded by all Central agencies concerned and State Governments because while the Look East Policy has yielded few returns to the Region thus far, it is in North East India that South-East Asia begins and, as such, it is for the North East to be enabled to play the arrow-head role in the further evolution of this Policy. This requires a redefining of the Look East Policy to resolve outstanding issues of trade, transit and investment with the countries neighbouring the region. [50]

Some important infrastructure initiatives have also been launched to promote Northeast regional trade with neighbouring countries. The Asian Highway Link, Asian Railway Network and a Natural Gas Pipeline Grid projects under active consideration of BIMSTEC have tremendous implications in removing the communication isolation of the region. While the Northeast will have access to the Asian Highway through the Imphal–Tamu feeder road, the railway systems of India and Myanmar are planned to be linked at the Dibrugarh railhead, which will give the region access to the Asian Railway Network. India constructed a road in 2001 in Myanmar linking the township of Tamu with the railhead at Kalemyo which connects Mandalay, the commercial hub of Myanmar. There is a proposal to construct a 1,360 km trilateral highway from Moreh (India) to Mae Sot (Thailand) through Bagan (Myanmar). [51] The rebuilding of the Stilwell Road, the road from Assam's Ledo to the Myitkyina in Myanmar to Kunming, which has a potential to connect Northeast India with the entire Southeast Asian nations, is also in the proposal stage.

Inspite of existing potentialities, not much work has been done in the region. Several factors have been identified which seem to impede greater linkages such as: insurgency networks and their role in creating parallel economy in nexus with collaborating agents; lack or failure of governance; poor literacy levels (except in Mizoram); inadequate infrastructure including poorly maintained roads and railway networks which often get targeted by insurgent groups also; borders being vulnerable to insurgent activities and contraband trade particularly drugs; narrow product base for border trade in the region which has led to fall in demand. (Officials claim that border trade through Champai (Mizoram) has dropped to 20 per cent and through Moreh (Manipur) to 10 per cent); the Inner Line Regulation of 1873 and the Restricted Area Permit (RAP) required for foreigners to gain entry to states like Arunachal, Manipur, Nagaland, etc, continue to affect free movement of people across the region. [52]

To remove popular apathy and hostility, there has to be an emphasis on indigenous knowledge systems coupled with a sense of economic and social justice. Once that happens, people support for 'Look East' could be guaranteed and the implementation smoother if not easier.[53]

Logically, India's 'Look East Policy' will have limited value if it does not have any impact on the region. The 'Look East Policy' begins with Northeast because it shares direct land borders with East and Southeast Asian neighbours. However, as far as the region is concerned, the policy has remained a talk shop and has not as yet evolved into a concrete policy with Northeast's neighbours and the greater South East Asian sub-region. Thus, despite the 'Look East Policy', the Northeast remains under economic captivity within the mainland Indian economy and its international borders.[54]

Evolving a Long-term Strategy Based on Human Security Paradigm?

Given the wide variety of issues and challenges which the 'Look East Policy' is supposed to deal with, it seems to be difficult to evolve a coherent strategy. In this connection, one scholar has recently argued that the Indian 'Look East Policy' making is influenced by three visions: (a) projection of Look East as an external security trajectory; (b) a strategy of economic cooperation and, (c) communitarian vision aimed at absorption of versions of sub nationalism in Indian Northeast and other connected regions.[55] The scholar goes on to argue that:

It seems that the Indian government wants the 'best-of-all' kind of an approach, resulting in uneasy compromises, awkward bottlenecks and policy indecisions. This trend is expected to continue till there is a conscious articulation of the underlying conceptual map to guide India's Look East policy to its desired destination.[56]

The 'Look East Policy' is linked up with global and regional trends and is coordinated with other policy options and initiatives. Global developments in the post Cold War period have presented both opportunities and threats. Re-engagement with Asia has assumed importance in the aftermaths of the global recession which has particularly affected the Western world. Rising importance of G-20 replacing G-8 as the main global decision making body in recent years and the enhanced prestige of India in global sphere as a 'rising power' has had its impact in 'Look East Policy' formulation also. East Asian leaders have often traced India's 'Look East Policy' to the diplomatic realism of former Prime Minister P.V. Narasimha Rao at a time of national crisis in the 1990s. Against this background, a dominant view in East Asia today is that the Indian Prime Minister Dr. Manmohan Singh is setting the terms for India's long-term engagement with key regional powers. Inevitably, such diplomacy will extend beyond the economic realm. India's strategic calculations are easily discernible too.[57] Within the Asia–Pacific region, there is a growing approval and demand for India playing a more assertive regional role. According to one regional leader, for instance:

India has been "Looking East" for almost two decades now. Here, I encourage India to define its neighbourhood to the East more broadly to include Southeast Asia...If India goes beyond merely "Looking East" to proactively "Engaging East" in a strategic manner, then the region will be more balanced. [58]

Greater engagement, however, requires greater commonalities. The new phase of Indian 'Look East Policy' should perhaps focus more on this search. This would not only involve piece meal removal of irritants like for instance, the issue of ill-treatment of Indian community members particularly in countries like Malaysia, or trade and service related disputes, but would also involve searching for new paradigms of cooperation involving consensual and cooperative approach to a range of issues concerning holistic development and traditional and non-traditional security issues. In this connection greater focus on evolving a common and cooperative human security agenda through consensus building could be one positive development. Some scholars, in this connection, have already began to focus on efforts to arrive at a more unified *security problematique* for their own region of concern i.e., Southeast Asia. Such linkages, according to the authors, can be seen in growing convergence in four areas: (a) area of conflict prevention; (b) approaches towards reducing the vulnerability of the security subject; (c) the third linkage evolving around the problem of who is to be governed and who is to be secured; and finally, (d) the fourth linkage relates to the ongoing crisis of collective security in both a regional and international context.[59] Another author has suggested that efforts should be made to 'Asianize' the paradigm of human security in order to make it more appropriate for the regional application.[60]

As one scholar notes:

For India, therefore, there is once again an opportunity to relate to Asia to its east. However, so far our diplomacy has been desultory, at best sporadic and episodic. Greater, consistency, greater commitment to open more trade and investment relations and a willingness to share in the region's problems and not just in its prosperity will help India move closer. [61]

Forging 'Look East Policy' initiatives on the basis of a human security paradigm could be a positive and holistic development in this regard. The most unique feature of this new concept is its incorporation of socio-economic development within a framework of security discourse, thereby making both concepts more holistic and acceptable to the international community. Human security, in this connection, has emerged as a political leitmotif or guiding vision for policy framing in many nation-states trying to evolve their foreign policy agendas which would be more suitable in grappling with myriad security related issues in the post Cold War world. It has been argued that in order to emerge as a successful guiding vision, a political leitmotif requires to fulfil three functions: (a) explanation and orientation; (b) coordination and action related decision guidance; and (c) motivation and mobilisation.[62] More specifically, it must be noted whether the concept has been sufficiently internalized by the policies, if not yet practices, of states to such a degree that it has taken on the shape of a doctrine capable of governing the future direction of state action. In spite of general global consensus achieved over the necessity of ensuring human security for the global population, developing a specific human security agenda as a part of a country's foreign policy goal, fit to be implemented, continues to be a difficult task. The projection of human security as 'freedom from fear and freedom from want' is perfect as an ideal to be achieved but continue to remain too abstract as a policy to be implemented, particularly by nation-states in their capacity as international actors.

One country that has taken much initiative, especially since the 1990s, to evolve a human security agenda and popularize and implement it through its foreign policy has been Canada. The Canadian approach though not widely divergent from the UNDP (United Nations Development Programme) approach towards human security, nonetheless, includes some more specific 'state-centric' security-related issues falling within the ambit of traditional security. Canada through her efforts to address global issues through multilateral forums such as the UN also was instrumental in creating more specific forums dealing with 'human security' issues. Such significant steps included the signing of the Lysoen Agreement with Norway in 1998 with its emphasis on enhancing human security, promoting human rights, strengthening humanitarian law, preventing conflict, and fostering democracy and good governance. Canada also made pioneering efforts to set up the Human Security Network (HSN) in 1999. In the Asian context, Thailand from Southeast Asia is a member of this network. Japan, in particular, has also been particularly successful within Asia in adopting a human security-oriented foreign policy. These have been, however, exceptions.

Concluding Remarks

The debate on human security is relatively new to Asia in spite of the historical heritage of traditional pre-colonial philosophies concerned with statecraft highlighting the importance of state sponsored welfare activities. As most nation-states within the continent have emerged as independent entities as a result of the decolonisation process since the end of the second World War, and are still struggling with the process of nation building, state-centric security paradigm still continue to be dominant in the foreign policy formulations of the governing elites. Multilateral and normative concepts of security have not found much resonance in Asia.

The possibilities of India developing a foreign policy agenda based on its conceptualisation and interpretation of human security would therefore involve much difficulties. New developments since the end of the Cold War and globalisation-related inter-linkages, have, however, generated fresh opportunities for India to come out of the state centric straitjacket mentality and give more scope to consensual and multilateral dimensions of foreign policy framing. At the global level also Indian bilateral and multilateral engagements, which have become much extended in recent years, also continue to focus on peaceful and consensual approach towards various issues. Though Indian foreign policy making process does not yet specifically use human security as a defining goal, much of the issues it is concerned with do fall within the agenda of human security. 'Look East Policy' making, in particular, offers scope for adoption of the human security agenda. Whether Indian policy makers would be willing to take up the challenge or display enough dexterity in implementing it, however, remains doubtful.

Notes

1. Some latest representative works include: Frederic Grare and Amitabh Mattoo (eds.), India and ASEAN - The Politics of India's Look East Policy. (New Delhi: CSH-Manohar-ISAS, 2001); Frederic Grare and Amitabh Mattoo (eds.), Beyond the Rhetoric: The Economics of India's Look East Policy, (New Delhi: CSH-Manohar, 2003); Prakash Nanda. Rediscovering Asia: Evolution of India's Look-East Policy. New Delhi: Lancer, 2003; Thingnam Kishan Singh (ed.), Look East Policy & India's North East: Problems and Perspectives, (New Delhi: Concept, 2008); Sunanda K. Datta-Ray, Looking East to Look West: Lee Kuan Yew's Mission India, (New Delhi: Penguin; ISEAS, 2009); R. Sen, T. Chakraborti, Anindyo J. Majumdar & S. Chatterjee (eds.), Power, Commerce and Influence: India's Look East Experience, (New Delhi: Lancers, 2009).

2. Walter C. Ladwig III, 'Delhi's Pacific Ambition: Naval Power, 'Look East', and India's Emerging Influence in the Asia-Pacific', *Asian Security*, Vol. 5, No. 2, 2009, p. 94.
3. S. D. Muni, India's 'Look East' Policy: The Strategic Dimension, ISAS Working Paper No. 121, Institute of South Asian Studies, University of Singapore, 1 February 2011, p. 2.
4. 'India-ASEAN Relations', India Perspectives, October 2010, Ministry of External Affairs, Government of India website (http://meaindia.nic.in/mystart.php?id=8901) (accessed: 18 February 2011).
5. 'The Rise of China and India: Southeast Asians Perceptions and Interpretations, Presentation of Dr. Hank Lim, Singapore Institute of International Affairs, JETRO-SIIA Workshop, Singapore, 13 April 2006, p. 11.
6. G. V. C. Naidu, 'Whither the Look East Policy: India and Southeast Asia', *Strategic Analysis*, Vol. 28, No. 2, April–June 2004, p. 333.
7. Sugata Bose, A Hundred Horizons: The Indian Ocean in the Age of Global Empire, (U.S.A.: Harvard University Press, 2006), p. 16.
8. Fernand Braudel, The Perspective of the World Civilization and Capitalism, 15-18 Century, Vol. 3, (U.S.A.: Fontana Press, 1985), p. 484.
9. For a traditional view on colonial disruption see for instance, K. M. Panikkar, India and Indian Ocean: An Essay on the Influence of Sea Power on Indian History (London: George Allen & Unwin, 1962); For an alternative viewpoint, see for instance, Michel Morineau, 'Eastern and Western Merchants from the Sixteenth to the Eighteenth Centuries', in Sushil Chaudhury and , Michel Morineau (eds.), Merchants, Companies and Trade: Europe and Asia in the Early Modern Era (Cambridge: Cambridge University Press, 1999), pp. 116–144.
10. Hari Vasudevan and Anjan Sarkar, 'Colonial Dominance and Indigenous Response', in Jayanta Kumar Ray (ed.), History of Science, Philosophy and Culture in Indian Civilization, Vol. 10, Part 6, Aspects of India's International Relations 1700-2000: South Asia and the World, (New Delhi: Pearson Longman, 2007), p. 29.
11. Cited in A. Appadorai (ed.), Select Documents on India's Foreign Policy and Relations: 1947–1972, Vol. 1, Oxford University Press, New Delhi, 1982, p. 21.
12. Ashok Kumar Mukhopadhyay, 'Ideological and Institutional Focus of Independent India', in Jayanta Kumar Ray (ed.), op. cit., p. 107.
13. S. D. Muni, op. cit., p. 6.
14. Ibid, p. 7.
15. M. G. G. Pillai, 'India and South-East Asia: Search for a Role', *Economic and Political Weekly*, Vol. 30, No. 30, July 1995, p. 1911.
16. For details see Kripa Sridharan, The ASEAN Region in India's Foreign Policy (USA: Dartmouth Publishing Co, 1996) cited in S. D. Muni, op. cit., p. 7.
17. S. D. Muni, op. cit., p. 8.
18. '60 Years of Independence: India's Foreign Policy Challenges', Address by Special Envoy to Prime Minister Mr Shyam Saran at the conference by the Institute for South Asian Studies, Singapore, 30 August 2007, p. 5(http:// www. isas. nus. edu. sg/ Attachments/ PresentationMaterial/ 20070830%20-%20Shyam%20Saran_23102009131408.pdf (accessed: 24 February 2011).

19. Source: Table 26, Foreign direct investment net inflow to ASEAN from selected partner countries/regions http://www.asean.org/stat/Table26.pdf (accessed: 27 February 2011).
20. Source: Department of Industrial Policy and Promotion, Ministry of Commerce and Industry, Government of India, http://dipp.nic.in/fdi_statistics/india_FDI_December2010.pdf (accessed: 27 February 2011).
21. (http://biz.zeenews.com/budget2011/story.aspx?newsid=139)(accessed: 26 February 2011).
22. Geethanjali Nataraj, 'Asean, India and the Free-Trade Game', Jakarta Globe, October 28, 2010(http://www.thejakartaglobe.com/commentary/asean-india-and-the-free-trade-game/397342) (accessed: 26 February 2011).
23. Source: http://www.eppo.go.th/inter/IOR-ARC/ior-arc.html (accessed: 27 February 2011).
24. Bay of Bengal Initiative for Multi-Sectoral Technical and Economic Cooperation Background, http://www.bimstec.org/about_bimstec.html (accessed: 27 February 2011)
25. S. D. Muni, op. cit., p. 14.
26. 'India–Singapore Relations', February 2011, Ministry of External Affairs, Government of India website (mea.gov.i n) (accessed: 17 February, 2011).
27. 'India–Malaysia Relations', January 2011, Ministry of External Affairs, Government of India website (mea.gov.in) (accessed: 17 February 2011).
28. 'India–Indonesia Relations', February 2011, Ministry of External Affairs, Government of India website (mea.gov.in) (accessed: 17 February 2011).
29. 'India–Thailand Relations', February 2011, Ministry of External Affairs, Government of India website (mea.gov.in) (accessed: 17 February 2011).
30. 'India–Vietnam Relations', February 2011, Ministry of External Affairs, Government of India website (mea.gov.in) (accessed: 17 February 2011).
31. 'India–Philippines Bilateral Relations', December 2010, Ministry of External Affairs, Government of India website (mea.gov.in) (accessed: 17 February 2011).
32. 'India–Laos Relations', February 2011, Ministry of External Affairs, Government of India website (mea.gov.in) (accessed: 17 February 2011).
33. 'Brunei', February 2011, Ministry of External Affairs, Government of India website (mea.gov.in) (accessed: 17 February 2011).
34. 'India–Cambodia Relations', February 2011, Ministry of External Affairs, Government of India website (mea.gov.in) (accessed: 17 February 2011).
35. 'India–Myanmar Relations', February 2011, Ministry of External Affairs, Government of India website (mea.gov.in) (accessed: 17 February 2011).
36. Ministry of External Affairs, Government of India, Annual Report 2009–2010, New Delhi, p. 20).
37. Rajiv Sikri, India's Foreign Policy Priorities in the Coming Decade, ISAS Working Paper No. 25, Institute of South Asian Studies, National University of Singapore, 25 September 2007, p. 21.
38. Amitendu Palit, India's 'Look East Policy': Reflecting the Future, ISAS Insights,

Institute of South Asian Studies, National University of Singapore, No. 96, 5 April 2010, p. 4.

39. Archana Pandya and David M. Malone, India's Asia Policy: A Late Look East, ISAS Special Report No. 2, Institute of South Asian Studies, National University of Singapore, 25 August 2010, p. 39.
40. Manjeet Singh Pardesi, Deducing India's Grand Strategy of Regional Hegemony from Historical and Conceptual Perspectives, Working Paper No. 76, Institute of Defence and Strategic Studies, Singapore, April 2005, p. 55.
41. Brian K. Hedrick, 'India's Strategic Defence Transformation: Expanding Global Relationships', The Leotart Papers, Strategic Studies Institute, US Army War College, p. 28.
42. Walter C. Ladwig III, op. cit., p. 95.
43. Ibid
44. Annual Report 2009–210, Ministry of Defence, Government of India, p. 37.
45. Ibid, p. 172.
46. Chietigj Bajpaee, **'India rediscovers East Asia', 31 October 2007, Asia Times Online,** http://www.atimes.com/atimes/South_Asia/IJ31Df02.html, **27 February 2011.**
47. Li Hongmei, 'India's "Look East Policy" means "Look to encircle China"?', People's Daily Online, 27 October 2010, http://english.Peopledaily.com.cn/90002/96417/7179404.html, (accessed: 16 February 2011).
48. Baladas Ghosal, Some New Thougts on India's Look East Policy, IPCS Issue Brief No. 54, Institute of Peace and Conflict Studies, New Delhi, October 2007, p. 1.
49. Press Statement by Shri Pranab Mukherjee, Minister of External Affairs after the Meeting on Look East Policy, October 31, 2007. http :// www.mea. gov.in/ mystart. php? id=100513267 (accessed: 8 December 2010).
50. North Eastern Region Vision 2020, Ministry of Development of North Eastern Region, North Eastern Council, 2008, pp. vi–vii), http:// mdoner.gov.in/ writereaddata/ sublinkimages/ Vision_2020. Pdf, (accessed: 26 February 2011)
51. Ibid, p. 275.
52. Namrata Goswami, Looking "East" through India's North East: Identifying Policy "Challenges" and Outlining the "Responses", IDSA Occasional Paper No. 2, Institute for Defence Studies and Analyses, New Delhi, June 2009, pp. 20–22.
53. Ibid, p. 22.
54. Dilip Gogoi, 'Introduction', in Dilip Gogoi (ed.), Beyond Borders: Look East Policy & North East India, (Guwahati & Delhi: DVS Pub., 2010), p. 5.
55. See, Shibashis Chatterjee, 'Conceptions of Space in India's Look East Policy : Order, Cooperation or Community?', in *South Asian Survey*, Vol. 14, No. 65, 2007, pp. 65–81.
56. Ibid, p. 80.
57. P. S. Suryanarayana, ;New economic idiom in Look East policy', The Hindu, 26 October 2010. http://www.hindu.com /2010/10/26/stories/2010102653291100.htm, (accessed: 16 February 2011).

58. Speech by Mr. Goh Chok Tong, Senior Minister at the Asia Society's 20th Asian Corporate Conference, 20 March 2010, New Delhi, India, p. 4 Source: http://www.siiaonline.org/files/ Senior.Minister.Goh.Chok.Tong.Speech.pdf, (accessed: 26 February 2011).
59. William T. Tow and Russell Trood, 'Linkages between Traditional Security and Human Security', in William T. Tow, Ramesh Thakur, and In-Taek Hyun, (eds.) Asia's Emerging Regional Order: Reconciling Traditional and Human Security, (New York: United Nations University), 2000 pp. 23–24.
60. Withaya Sucharithanarugse, 'The Concept of "Human Security" extended: 'Asianizing the Paradigm' in William T. Tow, Ramesh Thakur, and In-Taek Hyun, (eds.) op. cit., pp. 49–61.
61. Sanjaya Baru, Strategic Consequences of India's Economic Performance, (New Delhi: Academic Foundation, 2006), pp. 256–257.
62. For details see, Sascha Werthes and Tobias Debiel, 'Human Security on Foreign Policy Agendas: Introduction to Changes, Concepts and Cases', in Tobias Debiel and Sascha Werthes (eds.), Human Security on Foreign Policy Agendas: Changes, Concepts and Cases, INEF Report 80/2006, Institute for Development and Peace, University of Duisburg-Essen, 2006, pp. 12–13.